Contents . . . .

Introduction . . . .

FISHING happens to be one of our oldest surviving industries. Throughout the wild and rugged Scottish coast there remains ample evidence of the existence of fisher communities, even where none now exist.

Once thriving little hamlets clustered around safe inlets or sandy beaches but have long since been abandoned to nature's governing laws. During the herring bonanza of last century numerous creeks flourished and entire communities settled to establish a livelihood. Proof of this exists all over the coastal routes of the country.

However it is around the North and East coasts that this can be witnessed best. For there is hardly an inlet that does not have the mark of a fishing station or landing site. All the way from Peterhead to Buckie there is a rich vein of natural inlets transformed into well developed harbours where people became totally dependent on fish and coastal trading. However the vast majority were tidal harbours and although they served their purpose well in their day, it was towards the expanding deeper harbours, which became the principal ports, that the fishers grew more dependent on and especially as their fishing craft developed into much larger vessels.

It is ironic that an entire network of railways which played a very valuable role in transportation during the glorious years of the industry has completely disappeared; not only from the villages but from the four busy ports too. Landmarks have been left throughout the area to remind us of these heavy locomotives that performed a precious duty to our busy shores.

Although the old village harbours have been rejected for lack of deep water by fishermen, most have been put to good use by owners of pleasure craft. Then surprising as it may seem most of the fishers still live in their ancestral home villages and commute to the larger ports, making up a good majority of fishermen.

The hustle and bustle around these important Scottish fishing ports has never let up through the last two centuries.

Writers of old stated what a hard working, industrious class of people the fishers are. None could claim to alter their statements as one only has to walk around these ports, or enter the net stores to witness this fact today. It is not only the catching of fish but the preparation of the boats and gear before casting off from the pier and this involves long hard hours.

The horse drawn carts of distant memories have been replaced by articulated lorries and the old ways vanish with the new ideas, but what the future holds for continued success can only be determined by positive thinking accompanied with crystal clear vision and these port authorities have it.

The inclusion of the coastal villages is to illustrate their importance in the development of the four leading Scottish fishing ports.

The major economy of Northern Scotland springs from this region's busy ports. The days of the herring boom built our largest towns and the value of fish still maintains our economical strength.

What wealth there is circulating in Scotland today has its basis in Scottish waters. Some fish for oil while others for the sea's natural wealth, which shall remain long after the thick dark crude wears away.

Scottish fisherfolk are a special breed of people, strong in mind and spirit. Hardened by bitter weather and fierce gales they have become a proud race resolute in their employment.

TRIBUTE TO PETER BUCHAN

PETER never forgot the community spirit in Peterhead when he was a young lad and was most impressed with the following experience.

Two drifters returned to port with their entire fleet of nets wrecked. What was left of the nets was laid out at Battery Park where soon the area was black with fisherfolk patching and mending. Following this the embankment was crowded with South Bay women helping out. In fact nets were scattered all over the town being repaired and Peter was one of the boys that pushed barrow loads of nets to menders. Peter said: "It made me

Peter Buchan with his grand-daughter.
(Courtesy of Mrs Buchan).

prood tae be fisher seeing sik community spirit." In 3 days the two boats were back fishing.

Peter was proud of his fisher roots. His grandparents united two fisher communities, Burnhaven and Buchanhaven, when they were married; the wedding feast was hard fish. Peter himself was skipper of the Twinkling Star PD137 and after spending 30 years at sea, his fisher looks and fisher ways were always there. Years later J. R. Allan told him "Ye've saut water written a' o'er ye". He once suffered from herring fever which taught him a great deal about himself and others. "Ye think ye are gettin sae little fin ithers are gettin sae muckle. It's a cruel affliction an' it drives ye mad." One experience he enjoyed was listening to elderly men catching more herring at the harbour seats than they ever caught at sea. Peter's house "Mount Pleasant" was built 250 years ago by a sea captain named Andrew Fraser. His friends told him to burn it down as it was no use, but his determination proved them wrong.

Peter once told me, "Fin I'm writin' I like to write aboot folk. I like meeting folk. Ye see that's fit 'is life is a' aboot gettin' on wi' yer fellow men.

Peter Buchan will live on in the memories of North East folk through: his writing, his poetry, his story telling, but for those who witnessed his sermon in the broad Scots tongue, they will have sensed their roots both Scottish and Spiritual as never before.

PETERHEAD

IN 1593 the mould was cast for progress when Port Henry pier was built for the burgh of Peterhead. The lamp was certainly lit for a bright future in those far off days by those men of vision.

The selection of this area was an excellent choice, for the island of Keith Inch and the large natural anchorage have played a tremendous role in the build-up through the years. This point has been proved over the past fifteen years when Peterhead became the top white fish port in Europe, as well as a major offshore supply and repair base for the oil related industries.

Peterhead was once the leading European whaling station too. It began with the 169 ton Robert in 1788 and there were eight such vessels in 1815. One of the more successful years was 1814 when seven ships caught 164 whales. Greenland fisheries was the town's predominant industry during the first half of the nineteenth century.

Prior to 1831 Peterhead had a minimal involvement with the herring industry. In fact it was only when suspected cholera infected fishermen from Wick were refused entry to Fraserburgh that the fleet turned to Peterhead; from then this industry mushroomed at the Blue-toon.

The Arbuthnot museum, now the headquarters of North East of Scotland Museums has an excellent collection of artifacts, records and photographs related to the town's maritime history and is well worth a visit.

This extremely busy modern port has two separate authorities. There is the harbour authority and the Peterhead Bay Authority. While the former deals with everything within the harbour area the latter is responsible for the operations within the bay enclosure and much of this is oil-related business; oil supply vessels and oil rig repair berthing facilities. During the herring season numerous Russian factory ships take up anchorage within this sheltered enclosure. Peterhead is the most easterly deep water port in Scotland.

Harbour Street looking towards the Queenie.

Fishwives dividing the catch in 1890s.
(Courtesy of Peterhead Harbour Board).

Queen Street, Peterhead.

Albert Quay, opened 1990, is proving a valuable facility for fishing vessels and other trade. (Courtesy of Peterhead Harbour Board)

PETERHEAD DISTRICT

WHINNYFOLD stands firm above the high windswept Buchan headland. A narrow, well trodden footpath descends rather steeply to the cove where between 1855 to the fishing disaster in 1884, fifty-eight fishermen were employed.

CRUDEN BAY eighteenth century fishermen from the hamlet, Ward of Cruden, fished from the beach. Twenty-four boats attended the herring fishing here in 1855 and twenty years on there were sixty-eight. 1900 saw an end to the herring fishing from this harbour.

Golden Rod PD 10 leaving South Harbour.

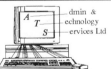

BULLERS O' BUCHAN a settlement of fishers used the cove below in 1792 and there was little change throughout the nineteenth century. The peak year appears to have been 1881 when twenty-four fishers used sixteen boats. It declined after this.

BODDAM this was a busy herring port last century. 1840 saw twenty-three herring boats working from the harbour but the year 1881 witnessed 151 drifters using this now busy harbour with thirteen curers resident in the village. Boddam declined soon after this while Peterhead reaped the benefits.

BURNHAVEN the old fishing village of Burnhaven has disappeared from the shore where in 1855 there were sixteen herring drifters and eight sma' line boats. 214 people were employed during the summer season that year. Even as late as 1881, 154 fishermen fished out of this small beach during the herring season. There was once a small harbour quay for landing and this was still in evidence a few years back.

BUCHANHAVEN in 1880 this village had 270 fishermen and around 90 boats. It may be interesting to note that from 1881 to 1883 Peterhead had 463 fishermen and 199 boats while Buchanhaven had 248 fishermen and 93 boats. Today the village and town have merged.

PD 182 enters South Harbour.

Fishing boat entering South Harbour today.
(Courtesy of Peterhead Harbour Board)

JIM BUCHAN

JIM BUCHAN has experienced life on board the old sail boats, motor boats and steam drifters and prides himself in recalling both name and numbers of the entire Peterhead fleet of steam drifters.

I first went to sea aboard John Noble Stephen's boat, the Sulevernia PD316 in 1914. She was a 70 foot Zulu, converted to motor with a 75 Gardner, but the skipper kept her sails which we used if the wind was favourable.

Peterhead had a tug we called the Flying Skud. She towed the sail boats out clear of South Bay and it was a bonnie sight to see them put up their sails. They had to be careful and not carry too much sail in wind. We were nearly caught while moving the sail as the wind changed direction; that was a frightening experience.

Both Carnegie and Irvine built modern wooden steam drifters in Peterhead. The Monkey Triple was the best steam engine. I'll always remember the Star of Faith PD222, she was a marvellous wooden built drifter; the fastest in Peterhead. You seldom saw a drifter break down as the engines were very reliable.

The old sail boats would have been fully loaded with 80 cran, but I can remember the steam drifter, Protect Me, come in with a record catch of 240 cran. Mind you they pushed the nets up forward to get the herring in. Then the motor boats Fruitful Bow with 320 crans and the Star of Bethlehem not far behind, held the Prunier Trophy; so the catching improved.

During both wars we were escorted to local fishing grounds. Admiral Simpson was in control during the first war and there was a large naval build-up in the South Bay. We could not leave port before sunrise and had to be back by sunset. South Bay entrance was guarded by patrol ships.

Times have changed and with modern advancements in boats and Peterhead harbour we have now the best fishing port in Europe.

BESSIE SIM

MY GRANDFATHER had the fishing boat Superior PD777 and he travelled to all the fishings as did my grandmother.

I was brought up by my auntie Mary Yule. Her husband, James, was lost in what we called the Peterhead pilot boat disaster in January, 1915.

My aunt was working in fish prior to that but after becoming a widow her life depended on it. There was a lot of trouble at the market among the men fish buyers who wanted the fish to themselves, but this deprived the widow women fish cadgers and there was no pension in these days. She finally got a permit in spite of the buyers. She got up at 3 o'clock in the morning and had the boiler going and the washing hung out before going down to the 6 o'clock fish market and then away with her creel. She often took a horse brake to Hatton in those days and then walked on a ten mile circular route.

She got permission from the council to put up a smoke house at 68 Roanheads. We used oak chips and sawdust from Dickies sawmill to smoke the haddocks. When there was no haddocks in Peterhead we got line haddocks from Rosehearty. I know that is amazing as this is the premier port now in Europe, but we often had to depend on Rosehearty line haddocks and they were valued at one penny more the pound. We cured our own fish and dried hard fish down there on the rocks, but then somebody had to keep watching them as the birds would have flown off with them; especially the gulls.

Auntie Mary then sold the shop and moved to what was always known as Brewery Brae, although Uphill Lane is its name. Well she married again and we continued to smoke fish. Then we began sending fish down to Glasgow, Manchester and London. The business expanded with first a horse drawn lorry and then three vans. Well they sold the Brewery premises in the 1950's and the police have got them now for garages. My auntie used to call them the Brewery without the brew. I'll always remember this coast was famous for cod but the best haddocks came from the Moray Firth.

Sandy Wood was the biggest curing station in Peterhead, but he lived in Deeside. I worked for them and it was a good firm to work for. Then there was Buchan's who had 5 crews and when I was with them they had Irish girls from Donegal who were beautiful singers and sang all the time they worked. Peterhead was a very busy town in those days which obviously laid the foundation stones for Europe's top fishing port.

BUCKIE

THE seventeenth century hamlet of Buckpool was the very beginning of Buckie.

Nether Buckie harbour was built by 1857 and 21 years later the Cluny Harbour was completed. From then, the race for the fishing grounds was on and the town thrived by leaps and bounds because of the developments in the industry; the population of Buckie swelled to 9000.

There were 480 Zulu sail boats here in 1900 and because of the fleet's growth a separate registration from Banff was required. Therefore in 1907 Buckie became a recognised port of registration when for the first time her letters BCK came into use.

Before the success of the steam drifter, Buckie's Star of Hope, a screw driven steamer, had been working since 1896 at the line fishing. By 1913 a third of the Scottish steam drifter fleet held BCK registrations and was second to the entire British fleet only by Lowestoft. The total number of registrations in that year was 698, out of which was 276 steam drifters; with the rest being sail or motor powered. Then to show how far advanced the Scots were in those days and in particular Buckie men, the entire Scottish fleet of steam drifters amounted to 884, while the English was merely 624. The following year Buckie had 298 steamers and still the largest fleet in Scotland.

In 1900 a steam drifter cost £2400 while a Zulu cost £700 and 8 years later the price rose to £3000 thus making the drifter an expensive buy. With that in mind few fishermen could afford these vessels. Whatever there was staunch support from this town, that largely depended on the fishing for its survival and to modernise the fleet was certainly a step in the right direction. This was not a case of partnership, but one of ownership and the

Left to right: Joe Herd, skipper of Ardelle, BCK 227, Sandy Sutherland, John Cowie, Edward Smith.

skippers won the support of local banks and other fishing related industries.

In 1920 Buckie men became leaders again when the Danish seine-net system was first introduced to Scottish fishers by them. During the 1920's Buckie owned the vast majority of seiners in the country.

The Buckie lifeboat Charles Brown.

Hustle and bustle at Buckie Harbour late last century.

Buckie steam drifter BCK 434.

PORTKNOCKIE

FOUNDED as a fishing community in 1677, it witnessed steady growth in the nineteenth century. 97 boats berthed within this sheltered refuge in 1840 and 1888 saw the development of a harbour. The year 1901 had 114 sail drifters at this harbour. Even in 1929 when most of the smaller harbours were deserted for larger ports as much as 58 steam drifters belonged here. 25 motor boats belonged here in 1957 with 14 of these over 40 feet in length.

One of this village's outstanding men was Joseph Mair, "Pim". It was on September, 1845, the year known as the disaster on the Moray Firth, when it was believed 2000 herring drifters were at sea.

A raging hurricane struck the unfortunate fishers and many perished. "Pim" was 33 and saw little hope but decided to use his mile long nets as a floating anchor. He secured his little craft with six of a crew on board to the nets and rode out the might of the gale over two days. He saved his craft, his men and his nets. "Pim's" technique of "riding the nets" was modelled by fishermen everywhere in severe storms.

FINDOCHTY

THERE is mention in a charter dated 1568, the year Findochty Castle was built, of a port and fishing grounds located here.

Findochty village was founded in 1716 when the laird encouraged Fraserburgh fisherfolk to settle down by the Broad Hythe. 39 boats used the landing area in 1842 and in 1901 as much as 119 boats harboured at the port. In 1957 Findochty fishers owned 30 motor vessels with 18 of these over 40 feet.

Shipbuilding took place here as in most of the inlets around the coast. For example a John Marshal was recorded here in 1851 and James Mair known as "Jimmy Bobbin" who built many Zulu boats. Herd and McKenzie began their building career at the Crooked Hythe in 1905 and launched their first steam drifter, the Bloomfield, BF218, in 1906. They continued their work at this site until 1918 and completed 32 launches of steam drifters, before moving their yard to Buckie.

PORTGORDON

THE ancient fishing hamlet of Gallochy and Port Tannachy vanished without trace when the fourth Duke of Gordon decided to build a new port and village in 1797.

In 1874 the Duke of Richmond replaced the old decaying harbour, which cost him £15,000. Over 70 boats used it in 1890's and 94 in 1914. While in 1920 there was a total of 61 boats; these were 20 sail and 8 motor and 33 steamers. In 1938 these figures had diminished to total 21.

Buckie's far better equipped port led to Portgordon's eventual demise, although as late as the 1930's white fish landings were still taking place.

CULLEN

THIS was a fishing settlement in the 17th century and to several accounts possibly much earlier. There were in fact 4 boats using this inlet in 1641 and two centuries later boat building was proving to be the predominant local industry alongside fishing itself. Cullen harbour was built in 1819 with another quay added in 1834. Cullen appears to have reached its peak in 1890 when 88 boats berthed here and yet in 1920 there were 27 steam drifters at Cullen; this at a time when many similar ports had faded out.

The railway line was opened in May, 1886 and marked one of the most outstanding pieces of construction by the G.N.S.R. with the spectacular viaducts.

VICTOR VASS

MOST of the people in the North-east depend on the fishing and the government could help the fishermen if they wanted to; but I don't think they do. You really think they want to end the fishing. Decommissioning is not the answer as all that is doing is putting people out of jobs. Then the quotas as they stand are not helping as there is no way anyone can meet their commitments. Again this is why fishermen are leaving the sea all the time.

Now the older class of boat has little future as the inshore fishing is on its way out as now you have to go further afield, some 70 to 130 miles every week to survive. When I came here 26 years ago there was a big fleet at Buckie working at the prawns, just two or three miles off. Everybody was getting a living then and the price was good, but I'm afraid that's all changed as the price of prawns has deteriorated over the last 20 years.

There may well be a future for a young lad going to the fishing, but he will have to go much further out to sea.

PETER SLATER

THE majority of Buckie steam drifters went to the fishing with some going to the anchor method of seine-net. This went on till the end of this type of seine-net in 1933. The local steam drifters fleet began to diminish after that.

Buckie was bad geographically placed in comparison to Fraserburgh, Peterhead and Stornoway for fishing; these were the ports the Buckie fleet landed. In the 1930's the nearest fishing grounds to Buckie were at Gamrie and latterly Clythness for herring.

There were a lot of activities in the old days. Preparation at the start of a season, with cart loads of nets and buoys and lorry loads of gear; then chaff beds. A change of a crew for the Yarmouth fishing meant a clean start.

There were three firms at Buckie that made canvas buoys. These were first cut, then shaped, before being filled with archangel tar to keep them watertight. Afterwards we used to paint them twice a year before going to the herring fishing — first in May and again in September.

Buckie had at least two net factories. They produced the cotton sheets for herring nets and a good number of women were employed in this. Fishermen then turned the sheets into net form in the winter months by adding corks and ropes then finally barking the nets.

After the second war, the seine-net arrived here and the 3 yards in Buckie became very busy. Soon the fleet became too big for the Moray Firth and new grounds were pioneered by Buckie fishermen. In 1961 Buckie skippers Jim Bruce and Alex Peem were involved with the introduction of prawn fishing. This was the beginning of what is called light trawling but I don't know about it.

IN THE OLDEN TIMES

IN THE old days Alex Addison used to walk the railway line from his home in Cullen to Buckie for a berth.

Later he owned the Catherine BF 404 and his brothers: William from Cullen, David from Findochty and James from Portknockie sailed with him. Alex was not superstitious but he did have some unfortunate experiences. He barked his nets on a Friday and that was regarded as a bad omen and when he bought the Catherine, a metal rabbit emblem adorned the mast top. All the locals pleaded with him to get rid of it but he never did.

Wherever, Alex never did well at sea and experienced

tragedy after tragedy. His boat would break down occasionally and once on the way to Wick to catch cod, the Catherine took fire at Clyth and sank; they lost everything. The last boat he was on the steering wheel struck him and the doctor treated him by rubbing strong liniment on his chest, but he died that night aged 53. The locals believed his misfortune was the result of his earlier action; but these were the days of superstition.

MACDUFF

MACDUFF took over the fishing district from the declining port of Banff in 1957. The area covered by B.F. registration extends from Crovie to Sandend.

In the old days of sail 100 trading vessels used the port and in 1890 there were 120 boats fishing out of Macduff. The first steam drifter to use this harbour was the Norseman, which was built by W. and G. Stephen, Greenbanks, Banff, in 1903; by 1914 there were forty similar craft out of a fleet of 82. The spring of 1921 saw boats with between fifty and sixty feet of keel at the seine-net. Although this type of fishing was gaining

At work on the mast of the Discovery at Macduff Shipyard. The Discovery is now berthed in Dundee as a museum.

Early stages of work on the Endeavour II in 1991.

popularity, herring by drift net was still being landed. There were also 21 sma' line fishing boats here in 1929 and therefore the port handled a complete range of fish caught by varying methods of fishing. 36 seine-net boats operated from Macduff in 1966, the year the fishmarket was built. Macduff still retains an active white fish fleet. Like most of the coastal towns, fish curing goes on near the sea front.

It may seem surprising that the major ports of Fraserburgh and Peterhead have lost their shipbuilding businesses but the smaller town of Macduff has retained its wooden class built yard and has progressed in recent years into the domain of the steel built class of vessels with remarkable success. It was here in the spring of 1993 that new masts were shaped out for Scot's Discovery now moored in Dundee as a museum.

Various marine services are based around the harbour to support the local fleet but like most ports all local business relies on the success of the fishing industry.

Endeavour II, a wooden built boat launched early 1993.

MACDUFF DISTRICT

CROVIE: In 1721 there was a small settlement of fishers and over a century later around 30 sma' line boats and 9 herring drifters used the shore here; they were manned with 100 fishermen. The number of craft increased to 60 by 1881, but began to dwindle after that time.

GARDENSTOWN: Fishers used this refuge in the 17th century and in 1720 Garden of Troup founded the village. Herring fishing started here in 1812 a little earlier than most areas along the coast. A total of thirty-nine boats used the landing area in 1839 and 51 years later there were ninety-two. 1929 saw a decrease in numbers although they were by then larger craft; out of 48 boats locals owned around 18 of them were steam drifters.

BANFF: This was a trading town since 1372. A total of thirty-two vessels belonged to Banff in 1797. Shipping docked at the banks of the river Deveron until the harbour was built in 1775. Although Banff developed into an important herring port in the 19th century it rapidly declined in the 20th century.

WHITEHILLS: A fishing settlement existed at Inverboyndie in the 15th century and just around Kinloch Head fishers were at work by 1624 on the site of the present day Whitehills. 7 boats used the old creek in 1797 and 51 craft were busily employed in 1855. 1890 saw some 98 fishing boats uses this old creek. It was in 1900 that the harbour was built and since those days a small fleet has continued to fish from here. This happens to be the only village within these four fishing districts that still retains a modern white fish fleet.

PORTSOY: Portsoy was erected into a burgh of barony by Mary Queen of Scots in 1550. This became a main fishing and trading port for many long years. Much evidence of this can be seen around the old harbour as many of the ancient buildings remain. In fact this was the first harbour built on the Banffshire coast and was completed in 1693.

The Port of Soy was an important Moray Firth trading and fishing port in the old days, with 37 ships owned locally. The year 1875 was extremely busy when 45,000 barrels of herring were cured in the town. 57 fishing boats used the harbour in 1881 and in 1936 there were 41 and out of these were ten steam drifters. After World War II Portsoy's remarkable days of fishing and trading had ended.

SANDEND: Known better as 'San-eyn' started as a fishing settlement in 1692. However it was in 1833 when the tiny harbour was constructed to shelter sma'line boats. 86 fishermen crewed 35 boats at Sandend in 1901 and two locals owned steam drifters in 1929.

GEORGE McKAY

GEORGE McKAY left the sea to become assistant harbourmaster at Macduff at the age of 55 years. Later he became the first fishing skipper to become harbourmaster, as previous to George's appointment the post was held by a merchant sea captain ticketholder.

George recalls his early years: "When I became a fisherman in the thirties, Macduff harbour was packed with steam drifters. A harbour badly in need of deepening as the boats were aground most of the time. There was no fish market then but fish were landed and sold at the Shore Street quay, on the edge of the town's main road. Since then I have seen the local fleet turn to boats of 40 and 50 feet and again today see them range from 60 to 80 feet. These craft have all the modern facilities, with the crews working under enclosed conditions. The boats filled with the latest fish finding and direction finding equipment and using a harbour where they are afloat despite the tides.

Life at the Ska, a fishing ground some 3 or 4 miles west of Rosehearty, began for me in the early years at sea and I spent 25 years on this fishing ground catching mainly lemon sole, sometimes even on the darkest nights, before having any help with Decca to find a position. All this was done by depth of water and the position of certain lights at Rosehearty. For example the pier and lighthouse and some lights that were switched off in the town helped give us precise markings. My boat at this time was the Incentive B.F. 40. She was well known amongst others fishing on the Ska.

I'll never forget I spent some time towing from the shall' water at Rosehearty out to the deep for a spell and I worked awa'. Then I changed to shootin' into the deep towing to the shall' towards Rosehearty and from that day I never looked back.

WILLIE HAY

ONE OF the best known figures within the fishing industry over the past 20 years is Willie Hay of Portsoy.

He was described during the 1975 Blockade as "the ultimate militant that got away with not appearing a militant". During his years at the helm of discussions with countless politicians, both at home and abroad, he was noted for his level head, clear reasoning and above all sincerity.

Recently retired as President of the Scottish Fishermen's Federation, a post held for 11 years, and with an MBE and CBE to his credit, this gentle giant gave up some of his leisure time to talk to us.

I was born in Finechty in 1929 and brought up in "San-eyn". We lived in a small cottage just at the head of the harbour. There was no inside toilet and we had to carry fresh water. My folks were very poor but so was everyone else at that time. Father owned a wooden steam drifter called 'Industry' which worked from Buckie, but ironically he made more money as a commander in the navy during the war than he did at the fishing. I can still see him yet catching that train at Sandend station when he left for the war.

All I ever thought about was the sea and fishing. I went for two years at the drift net on steam drifters. The Olive Tree was one and I was with Fred on the Incentive at the Broch. After that I went seine-net as that was the thing then. In 1954 I got my skipper's ticket and got the Golden Eagle, followed by the Lone

Star and I finally built the Illustrious at Thomsons. She was a 70 foot seine netter and I did very well with that boat and retired from her in 1984.

I used to take an interest in the politics of fishing. In 1971 the skippers moved out of Aberdeen to Peterhead and that was probably the best move we made and Peterhead Harbour Board at that time were marvellous. First we landed on the quays but they built this large modern market and we never looked back. In 1975 we had the Blockade, when we decided to block imports. This took place all along the coast and I was in charge at Buckie and finally made chairman of the Blockade Committee. I remember in Aberdeen, Andrew Strachan of the Challenger did a great job, but then they all did. Before the Blockade we never got to speak to the government ministers, but this action altered that. Soon after I suffered a heart attack and when I improved I was made chairman of the White Fish Producers.

I have never been to sea on a Sunday, that is until one day after a spell of bad weather I decided to go out. Leslie Mair and the Margaretta from Buckie was alongside and I remember when I was going to shoot my gear I cried to Leslie, "I dinna ken fit tae dee oot here on a Sunday." "I'll tell ye fit tae dee Willie Hay. Jist ye throw awa yer dan an' switch on the radio an' listen tae the service," that was his answer.

I was a skipper for 30 years and I had the same mate and most of the crew all that time. I loved going to the sea. I found it a great challenge. I had a contented life. If I lost a net at sea I did not let it bother me.

The Scottish Fishermen's Federation was founded in 1972 with Gilbert Buchan as President and I came in as vice-president in 1978 and took over as President in 1982 when Gilbert retired. I was there when Peter Walker signed the Common Fisheries' Policy at Brussels in 1983. There was nothing wrong with this policy as there was a good 5 or 6 years fishing, It only started going wrong when the quotas were cut in 1989-90; that's when the problem arose.

I started fishing and saw the very poor times and appreciated it when the good times came. I think the fishermen are a good breed of lads. There is nobody under more stress than they are during a force 10 gale. I lived in a council house until I built this one and now I can watch the bad weather and the good weather and I love it, just looking out to sea. The sea has been my whole life and I have totally enjoyed it.

Sheila and Willie Hay, Past President Scottish Fishermen's Federation.

FRASERBURGH

FRASERBURGH, better known as the Broch, which had its beginnings in the sixteenth century, is a fishing town to the core.

The port of Fraserburgh rapidly ascended into a leader for carrying out fisheries, marketing, curing and exporting of herring. During the herring season of 1879, as much as 844 sailing drifters harboured here and in 1914 a fleet of 230 steam drifters belonged to Fraserburgh and district. The Broch has always been a trading as well as a fishing port and a large fleet of trading ships were based here too.

This is one of the country's premier fishing ports which has the advantage of being backed up with a huge local owned industrial force, all geared up for modern fishing and trading requirements.

There is a large pelagic and white fish fleet stationed at this port and approximately 20 fish factories with a new one to meet the needs for pelagic fish is in the process of being built at the newly deepened basin for the deep water fleet.

Fraserburgh Harbour.
Courtesy of the Harbour Board.

Fraserburgh was primarily a herring fishing town in the early days. Kippering was big business at the Broch not that many years ago, but with the closure of the herring fishing grounds to conserve stocks, this particular industry faded away.

However the herring industry has awakened again in recent years and although the pelagic fleet may be smaller than that earlier this century the boats are much larger and their gear have tremendous capabilities. Russian factory ships are a common sight during the herring season here and last year heralded another big fleet within the Bay at Fraserburgh.

Fraserburgh Harbour last century (Courtesy of Robert Wiseman).

Crew of Andra Tait FR 226.

Crew of the Unity FR 248.

The Reaper FR 958 from the Scottish Fisheries Museum, Anstruther, with L. Forbes and two members of the crew.

Crew of the Ocean Surf FR 225.

38

Crew of the Craigearn.

Sail boats leaving port (Coutesy of Robert Wiseman).

FRASERBURGH DISTRICT

ST COMBS: The three following communities referred to jointly as Inver-St-Cairn provided an enormous contribution to Fraserburgh's fleets, both past and present. In the year 1881 for example, residents owned 142 boats.

INVERALLOCHY: The two following villages of Inverallochy and Cairnbulg have retained perfectly the character of old seatowns with their houses gable end on to the sea. In 1855 a total of 78 boats used the old boat shore and by 1881 the villagers possessed 126 boats.

CAIRNBULG: Fishermen here owned 52 boats in 1855 and 97 by 1881. A small harbour was constructed to the west of this village in the 1920s, but both Inverallochy and Cairnbulg contributed largely over the years to the development of fishing in Fraserburgh.

SANDHAVEN: It was at the sandy beach, or sand haven, that the harbour serving both this village and Pittulie was built. Forbes Shipbuilding once employed 50 men but only a few remain now and they are involved in ship repairs.

PITTULIE: This hamlet's links with fishing dates back to 1570 and its old creek lies unaltered from the days boats were drawn up on its pebbled shore.

ROSEHEARTY: Fishing goes back to the 14th century here. The port of Pitsligo, now Port Rae, was in existence by 1509, probably due to the Forbes's of Pitsligo who were in residence from 1423. The herring fishing developed here in 1810. In 1829 the town had 44 herring boats and in that same year Peterhead had only 12. The 1870s saw 130 herring drifters berthing at the two harbours.

Loading groceries aboard Cairnbulg boat FR 150 - Left to right; John Duthie, Arthur Buchan, Gordon Cooper and Gilbert Green.

Duchess of Kent inspects the Sea Cadets at Fraserburgh Harbour.
(Courtesy of Mrs Delmaestro).

Robert Wiseman displays his photo collection at Fraserburgh Deep Sea Mission.

Gamrie boat Jacinth BF 437. Crew members Ernest West, Barry Ritchie, Alex Watt and John Cowe stretching the wire ropes.

PENNAN

PENNAN lies between the breathtaking heads of Troup and Auchmedden. This was once the haunt for smugglers and the area is steeped in their adventurous tales.

There existed a small harbour in 1742 which was devastated by storms 50 years later. A new harbour was built in 1845 and by 1855 the community owned 15 herring drifters and 25 smaller craft. The 1870s saw a total of 300 people employed in the herring fishing at Pennan. However 60 years later there were only 5 sma' line boats although one local man owned a steam drifter which was harboured elsewhere.

JOCK SMITH

FIN WE wis bairns we wis aye up in the net room either fillin' the needles or rowin' twine on to the rolls fae the hanks; as youngsters we wir aye oot at nicht fishin'.

My auld diddie 'Chappie' nivir referred to yowels as baldies bit he aye cad them Garabaldies. Now whither this class name wis teen fae the Italian General I dinna ken.

The Blighty wis an 80 foot Zulu built in 1904. In my teens an auld man telt me "see at boat ye're on, weel at een made th' fastest run fae Yarmouth tae Cullen 'at wis ever kent. Aye she wis an afa fast boat in her sail days." She hid twa sixty H.P. Kelvins in my day and went tae th' Broch an' sometimes Wick. She wis sold tae Finechty around the war.

Rosehearty smacks were bonnie boats with roon starns bit the last een o' th' auld motorised sailboats gan oot o' th' Broch wis the Victoria. I mine fin the Macduff skiffs, as we cad them, came in the go, 50 feet wi' cruiser starns. They wint tae the seine-net an' herrin' fishin' at hame in the summer. A weel bit they grew bigger tae.

I feenished up gan seine-net a' th' year roon. I flogged a' ma' herrin' nets in the sixties fin th' drift-net deet oot. Maist o' them wint to cover strawberry plants as they wir worthless.

George Sutherland.

GEORGE SUTHERLAND

BEING born and brought up in Portsoy was a sure mould for shaping the future of a successful fisherman.

George's father had the steam drifter Val and pursued the seine-net fishing which he in time went to.

I left the school when I was fourteen-and-a-half when the herring was about to start. All the local boys wanted to go to the summer herring fishing and the result was a class of girls and one boy when the school resumed; but all the boys had to return to school, so there was a lot of glum faces there. That was how it was in a seatown. My first spell at sea ended with me having to go to bed to regain control over my feet.

I was only at the drift net for two nights for the experience and followed my father to the seine-net in 1948. This was in the 40 foot Remembrance father bought from Pittenweem after the war. Then he got the 52 foot Windsor and spent a longer period at sea landing in Wick. Our friends were horrified when we had not arrived back at Fraserburgh and a search was mounted. After an all night search we were not very popular as the search parties had lost their Saturday night while we were comfortably berthed at Buckie.

In 1958 we built the Remembrance, a 63 foot state of the art seine-net boat at £14,000, which was built at Thomsons of Buckie. My father was skipper for only six months before he died and at 23 years of age I was thrown in as skipper. The Remembrance was a modern seine-net boat and we did well in her. After 18 years we bought the six-year-old Stand Hope from Peterhead and changed her name to Sans Peur. Now lots of people ask what it means, well actually it is the motto of the clan Sutherland. She has been modernised and kept up to date and it's been a good boat for us.

Before the advent of 'Blackfish' we won the Maitland Trophy for landing the most white fish into Fraserburgh for 13 consecutive years. There has been far better boats but they landed in Peterhead or Aberdeen but we had the highest grossing up until two years ago.

The Maitland Trophy was put up to encourage people to land in Fraserburgh, to bring money into the port to generate around the tradesmen and industries of Fraserburgh rather than a one-off shot situation.

Whatever, after 44 years at sea I came ashore this last New Year. I enjoy the politics of the industry. We are not doing a great job, but we are doing our best.

George Sutherland is perhaps best known as:

The longest serving Harbour Commissioner at Fraserburgh; Chairman of the Fishermen's Benevolent Fund; Chairman of the Fraserburgh branch of the White Fish Producers; Chairman of the Scottish White Fish Producers representing 560 boats and recently Vice-President of Scottish Fishermen's Federation.

COALING THE DRIFTERS
Bill Macdonald

IT WIS seasonal work coalin' the drifters, an' a short day as weel. They cam' in for coal in the mornin' an' awa tae sea an' syne back the neest mornin' after burning that lot up.

It wis a' peace work. Usually 6 or 7 o' a squad consisting o' 3 humfers and 3 fillers. It wis a hard job, bit ha'in half a croon the ton, wis gye gweed money for 'at time.

Walkin' the plank wis the warst o't. I wis aye fortunate I niver fell bit I mine fin "Toxie" fell in the water doon the Sooth pier, aye we worked wi Baxter then. Ye hid tae hae a steady fit an' a level heed, or else ye could expect the hard deck or o'er the side.

If it wis low water ye could aim the top bunker fae the wheelhouse; so the plank wis fae the pier to the roof o' the wheelhouse. Noo if the tide wis low, syne ye hid a sloapin' plank, an' that wis difficult. It wis fin the plank moved oot when the boats floated fae their births at Yarmouth river 'at wis the worst experience I hid. Aye mony a humfer hid a drookin' 'ere.

PROMISING FUTURE
By John Wallace

A FEW years ago Fraserburgh Harbour Commissioners produced an information booklet entitled, "Fraserburgh a Port with a Promising Future".How prophetic those words have turned out to be. Since that publication, the most important event in the town's history occurred on June 22, 1992.

Her Majesty Queen Elizabeth accompanied by the Duke of Edinburgh officially opened our dry dock and ship repair facility and Inner Balaclava deepening. The dry dock has proved a boon to the larger pelagic fleet of vessels of which Fraserburgh boasts home port to over half the country's pursers. The smaller vessels can use the dry dock in tandem, thanks to the hydraulically operated rams.

Complementing the dry dock is the deep water berthage in the Inner Balaclava. This basin has been transformed from providing only 6ft. at low water to 21ft. and is therefore the deepest in the harbour. Finding grants of some 65% was procured from the Scottish Office towards the project which was geared to attract an onshore pelagic factory. With the obvious bonus of deep water, the Commissioners cleared a large site at the Balaclava (which included the old ice factory, Bill Taits and Charles Wills) in the hope of securing a developer.

In May of 1993 after very protracted negotiations, Dr Francis Clark of Scofish International, finally broke ground on a pelagic factory costing over £3 million. The vessels will be able to moor alongside the factory and discharge directly into it thus saving labour and more importantly preserving product quality. Looking to the future on this front, there remains an obvious need to extend a deep water channel from the Inner Balaclava all the way to the harbour entrance. This would make the harbour non-tidal for larger pelagic and commercial traffic. While Parliamentary approval exists to deepen the main Balaclava harbour it is unlikely that the associated additional costs would bring the Commissioners the extra funds needed to pay for such an undertaking.

Most of the foregoing has primarily been of benefit to the pelagic sector, although not exclusively. The Commissioners have built some of the most modern facilities to complement the 'white fish' or demersal fleet. With new chilled fishmarkets, deeper water berthage, hydraulic storm gates, these changes have attracted outside investment, such as the two new ice factories. Changes will continue to be made as and when necessary to keep the port at the forefront of a very high tech industry.

When contemplating new developments, one must be acutely aware of certain factors in the decision making process. Firstly, and obviously the question must be asked, is the development possible i.e. physically, financially, etc. Then is it feasible, i.e. in the economic climate or changes in business patterns; and then, is it desirable i.e. out of all the necessities within ones control, does this new development take precedence. Even if the answer is yes to all of these questions many other considerations must be made.

The Fraserburgh Harbour Commissioners have been guided by a development policy of a most exacting nature. The proper cost benefit studies have been conducted by professional bodies. These results have been tabulated with our own data and presented to the Scottish Office for grant assistance. Any capital works requiring Parliamentary approval has been fastidiously pursued to gain the proper collateral to enable development. It must be remembered that should the commissioners default on their commitments then an outside body would effectively be in control of our harbour.

Balancing the needs of the port with current and projected finance while repaying existing loans all shape the decisions we make. If we continue to do this job correctly and if the twenty years are anything to go by, then our fishermen, our friends and our visitors who call the Port of Fraserburgh their home will enjoy the fruits of those promises the Commissioners made of progressive development based on financially sound principles.